IF WINNING WERE EASY, EVERYONE WOULD DO IT

IF WINNING WERE EASY, EVERYONE WOULD DO IT

Motivational Quotes for Athletes

Kim Doren and Charlie Jones

**Andrews McMeel
Publishing**

Kansas City

02 03 04 05 06 BID 10 9 8 7 6 5 4 3 2 1

Library of Congress Cataloging-in-Publication Data

Doren, Kim.
   If winning were easy, everyone would do it : 365 motivational quotes for athletes /
Charlie Jones and Kim Doren.
      p. cm.
   ISBN 0-7407-2702-8
   1. Athletes—Quotations. 2. Sports—Quotations, maxims, etc. I. Jones, Charlie,
1930- II. Title.
   GV707 .D67 2002
   796—dc21

2002066529

Book design by Holly Camerlinck

Attention: Schools and Businesses
Andrews McMeel books are available at quantity discounts with bulk purchase for educational, business, or sales promotional use. For information, please write to: Special Sales Department, Andrews McMeel Publishing, 4520 Main Street, Kansas City, Missouri 64111.

To Steve, Mark, and Cameron—three winners.
Even better, you're my brothers-in-law.
Thank heaven for sisters with good taste.

KIM

To Ira, Jonesey, Junior—three in one.
He's not heavy; he's my brother. I'm the heavy one,
and he's always carried me.

CHARLIE

INTRODUCTION

It's almost a given that when you enter any locker room, be it high school, college, or the pros, you'll be greeted by quotations on walls, in lockers, on mirrors—wherever space is available. They're ubiquitous.

Why? Because quotes offer inspiration. They are a succinct but effective way to help athletes prepare their minds so they can achieve their best. Words remind, uplift, and motivate. Most important, they can spark a fire in one's soul to reach a seemingly impossible goal.

We love quotes. We've been collecting them for years. Many come from the numerous interviews we conducted with successful athletes and coaches in the course of writing our books. For this book, we have selected quotes that will give you a better understanding of the mindset required to win, along with a better insight into the psyche of some well-known sports figures. Not only are many of these quotes inspiring, they're also quite entertaining.

It may seem as though the quotes in this book are solely about winning at sports—the preparation and training required, the character and attitude desired, the skills needed to overcome setbacks and obstacles. But these quotes can just as easily be applied to other realms of life, including business, family, and education. It's fine if you don't agree with some statements. Focus on the ones that bring meaning to you and use them to find the key to winning in *your* heart and mind. Our greatest hope is that the collective wisdom captured by these quotes will help you in your quest to become a champion.

IF WINNING WERE EASY, EVERYONE WOULD DO IT

It's not where you start
but where you finish.

APRIL HEINRICHS
Coach of the U.S. women's national soccer team

To be successful in anything, a person must always want to be better, not only than your opponent but better than your last performance. Done correctly, being competitive is a wonderful way to always try to be a better person by learning from your mistakes and capitalizing on your successes.

HALE IRWIN
All-time victory leader on the Senior PGA tour

My mom would never let us quit. She always taught us the importance of sticking with it, even when times are tough. We didn't just hear her, we watched her. I know what to do because she led the way. She showed us that if you put your mind to it, you can accomplish the world. No matter where you're from and what you're up against.

THEO RATLIFF

All-star center for the NBA Atlanta Hawks

Twenty seconds before a race, there's absolute focus. The key thing is to achieve relaxation, but at the same time you've got to have this absolute total control. You've got to find the balance between being totally ready to go and being really at peace with yourself as well.

CATHY FREEMAN

Australian who won the gold medal in the 400-meters in the 2000 Olympics

Always be
prepared to win.
That's what I focus on.
Keep working toward
perfection.

———

WILLIE DAVIS
Pro Football Hall of Fame member

You have to dream big and go for it. Surround yourself with people who believe in you and ignore those who try to bring you down. Never give up, no matter what—overcoming obstacles makes you stronger!

SHANNON MACMILLAN

U.S. Olympic and women's national soccer team star

You don't win
on emotion.
You win on execution.

———

TONY DUNGY

Head coach of the NFL's Indianapolis Colts

A true champion
knows how to overcome
doubts and manage those
doubts and turn them
into motivation.

MISTY HYMAN

*Olympic gold medalist in the 200-meter butterfly at the
2000 Sydney Games*

You've got to believe you can win. But I believe respect for the fact that you can lose is what you always have to keep in your mind so that nothing surprises you.

ANDRE AGASSI
Winner of all four tennis Grand Slams

I never wanted to be one of those people who looks back and says, "I wonder if . . ." If I have a goal, I'll go out and set forth to achieve it. When something is your passion, it becomes everything. You put everything into it without hesitation. No questions. No doubts. Nothing to stop you.

―――――

KIM FITCHEN

Cross-country runner and member of three U.S. World relay teams who never seriously ran or competed until she was twenty-five years old

My mind is my
biggest asset.
I expect to win every
tournament I play.

—————

TIGER WOODS
Number-one-ranked golfer in the world

I don't want to give anyone an edge in my mind. Every time I walk out on the court, I have to feel I'm the best so I can compete well. A lot of times, my chief rival is just me.

VENUS WILLIAMS
Winner of the U.S. Open and Wimbledon

onfidence is only born out of one thing—
demonstrated ability. It is not born of anything
else. You cannot dream up confidence. You cannot
fabricate it. You cannot wish it. You have to accomplish
it.

BILL PARCELLS
Former NFL head coach

S ingle-mindedness. I hate to say it because I don't think it's the best thing for developing a person, but the single-mindedness—just concentrating in that one area—that's what it takes to be a champion.

CHRIS EVERT
Hall of Fame tennis player

The key is
that I control my life;
my life doesn't
control me.

———

GABRIELLE REECE
Pro beach volleyball player

I am a winner.
I just didn't win today.

GREG NORMAN
Two-time British Open champion

I believe I'm one of the best pitchers in the world—I know I am as far as results go. But you can't live on your legacy. Every time I step on the mound I have to prove it.

MICHELE SMITH

U.S. Olympic softball team pitcher in 1996 and 2000

I f my dreams can happen to me, your dreams can happen to you. Champions are not made on the track or field; champions are made by the things you accomplish and the way you use your abilities in everyday life situations.

BOB BEAMON
Former world-record long jumper and track coach at Florida Atlantic University

I'd rather have more heart than talent any day.

―――――

ALLEN IVERSON

2001 NBA MVP of the Philadelphia 76ers

It's important to know that at the end of the day it's not the medals you remember. What you remember is the process—what you learn about yourself by challenging yourself, the experiences you share with other people, the honesty the training demands—those are things nobody can take away from you whether you finish twelfth or you're an Olympic champion.

SILKEN LAUMANN

Canadian Olympian who overcame injury to win a bronze and a silver medal in single sculls rowing in 1992 and 1996 respectively

I don't think you can ever will yourself to win. I think you prepare yourself the best you can, get yourself in the best mindset you can get in, and go after it.

JACK NICKLAUS
Six-time winner of the Masters

My mom gave me unconditional support and unfailing love. You can't get any better than that. That's why I've never been afraid to lose.

MIKE KRZYZEWSKI
Basketball coach of Duke University,
2001 NCAA champions

A winner will find a way to win. Winners take bad breaks and use them to drive themselves to be that much better. Quitters take bad breaks and use them as a reason to give up. It's all a matter of pride.

NANCY LOPEZ
LPGA Hall of Fame member

I keep telling my kids whether you achieve the goal or not is not the most important thing. Putting yourself in position to achieve those goals is what's important.

―――――

STEVE SCOTT
American mile record-holder and track coach at Cal State University–San Marcos

Every single day I wake up and commit myself to becoming a better player. Some days it happens, and some days it doesn't. Sure, there are games I'm going to dominate and there are going to be games when I struggle. But it doesn't mean I give up.

MIA HAMM

One of the all-time greatest women soccer players

To a winner, complacency and overconfidence can be destructive. To losers, desperation and despondency are just as harmful.

BILL WALSH
Former NFL and college head football coach

You have to be extreme to be exceptional. I couldn't revel in being number one. I had to get to zero. When my fitness was at its peak, I was intimidating. I made guys cave in. They'd be dejected in the locker room after matches, and I'd go out for a run, as if it wasn't enough. I'd rub it in their faces. I meant to do that.

JIM COURIER

Winner of four Grand Slam tennis titles

S et goals for things you can control. In my case, I can't control the marks from the judges, but I can control how I train every day, and I can control my performance.

CLAIRE CARVER-DIAS
Olympian on Canada's synchronized swimming team

I think competing is more important than winning. There have been a lot of times when I've teed it up and I didn't win but I felt like I competed. I felt like this was not my day, but I never gave up, and I tried on every shot, and then next week I'd go get them.

JULI INKSTER
LPGA Hall of Fame member

Success shouldn't be measured by how much you have but by how much you give back.

DANNY VILLANUEVA

Chairman of Bastion Capital Corporation
and former NFL placekicker

W hen I'm in a bout and I stop fighting to win and start fighting not to lose, I'm almost guaranteed to lose because I quit taking chances.

KELLY WILLIAMS
U.S. Fencing Association's 1998 Female Athlete of the Year

It's not so much what you accomplish in life that really matters, but what you overcome that proves who you are, what you are, and whether you are a champion.

JOHNNY MILLER
TV golf analyst and former U.S. Open winner

Winning doesn't always mean being first. Winning means you're doing better than you've ever done before.

—————

BONNIE BLAIR

Olympic gold medalist in speed skating

A lot of times the expectations of you are so high that no matter what you do you are never going to be able to live up to those expectations. So you better go out and do the best you can and enjoy it.

JOHN ELWAY

Former quarterback of the Denver Broncos and Super Bowl MVP

C ompetition in its best form is a test of self. It has nothing to do with medals. The winner is the person who gets the most out of themselves.

AL OERTER
Winner of four Olympic gold medals in the discus

I missed more than nine thousand shots in my career. I've lost almost three hundred games. Twenty-six times I've been trusted to take the game-winning shot and missed. I've failed over and over again in my life. And that is why I succeed.

MICHAEL JORDAN
Basketball legend

Success isn't winning every time. A lot of different factors go into every race, and you can't control all of them. Success means doing as excellent a job as you can on that particular day. The people I admire most aren't necessarily the most wonderful athletes. I admire the ones who keep coming back and doing it, time after time.

AIMEE MULLINS
Double-amputee track star

Winning is great, but it's the long road to get there that makes it worthwhile.

STAN SMITH
Tennis legend

Pressure bursts pipes. I thank God for giving me peace of mind to overcome pressure. The difference between winning and losing is when pressure hits.

EVANDER HOLYFIELD

Heavyweight boxing champion

You've got to have the guts not to be afraid to screw up. The guys who win are the ones who are not afraid to mess up. And that comes right from the heart.

———

FUZZY ZOELLER
Masters golf champion

I drew my strength
from fear. Fear of losing.
I don't remember the
games I won, only
the games I lost.

BORIS BECKER

*Three-time winner of Wimbledon
and youngest champion ever*

I am afraid of failure, but I think it's a good thing. If you're afraid, you'll do what you can not to fail. You learn from your failures. Everybody who is successful has failed at some time.

CHRIS WITTY

Olympic gold, silver, and bronze medalist in speed skating

You don't have to be better than everybody else, you just have to be better than you ever thought you could be.

KEN VENTURI

U.S. Open golf champion

You can't depend
on other people,
you have to run
your own race.

JOAN BENOIT-SAMUELSON

*Winner of the first women's Olympic marathon
in 1984 in Los Angeles*

Y ou only fail if you don't finish the game. If you finish you win. You have to measure what you started out with by what you overcome.

MIKE WEBSTER

NFL Hall of Fame center for the Pittsburgh Steelers

The moment of victory
is much too short
to live for that
and nothing else.

MARTINA NAVRATILOVA
Winner of 54 Grand Slam tennis titles

W hen someone tells me there is only one way to do things, it always lights a fire under my butt. My instinct is, "I'm going to prove you wrong."

PICABO STREET

*Olympic gold medalist in the Super G at
the 1998 Nagano Olympics*

B efore you move on, you've got to set a standard for the next person. I always knew my limitations. But I always knew my strengths. You play the cards you're dealt. You've got to play them. God doesn't deal bad hands.

HERMAN EDWARDS
Head coach of the New York Jets

You lose, you smile,
and you come back the
next day. You win,
you smile, you come
back the next day.

———

KEN GRIFFEY JR.
Cincinnati Reds baseball star

The spirit, the will to win, and the will to excel are the things that endure. These qualities are so much more important than the events.

VINCE LOMBARDI

NFL Hall of Fame coach

You're going to make
mistakes in life.
It's what you do after the
mistakes that counts.

BRANDI CHASTAIN
World Cup and WUSA soccer star

From what we get,
    we can make a living;
what we give, however,
    makes a life.

ARTHUR ASHE
Tennis Hall of Fame legend

The team with the best athletes doesn't usually win. It's the team with the athletes who play best together.

LISA FERNANDEZ

Star pitcher on the U.S. Olympic softball team
that won the gold medal in Sydney

I t's like an orchestra with many different instruments working to make one grand piece of music. Each player plays his own way, but only if it conforms to the larger objective.

LOU LAMORIELLO
NHL Devils general manager

One of the most awesome things about sports, particularly team sports, is that everything you need to do to be successful on the playing field carries over directly into life. In a team sport you have to learn how to work together, to set goals, and then work toward those goals in a productive way. You learn to be responsible and you learn how to not only depend on others, but also be independent so you can support others.

SHEILA CORNELL DOUTY
*U.S. Olympic first baseman on the 1996 and
2000 gold-medal-winning softball teams*

Team unity is important. When I talk to friends on Super Bowl teams, they always say they love coming to work. That's the sign of a winner.

TONY GONZALEZ

Pro Bowl tight end of the Kansas City Chiefs

When I'm on the field, I get an adrenaline rush that makes me think I cannot lose. I have so much energy running through me, I feel almost superhuman.

———

JULIE FOUDY

Captain of the U.S. World Cup and Olympic soccer teams

My coach told me, "Larry, no matter how much you work at it, there's always someone out there who's working just a little harder—if you take 150 practice shots, he's taking 200." And that drove me.

———

LARRY BIRD

Hall of Fame basketball player for the Boston Celtics

I asked my coach if I get extra credit for throwing up during a workout. He said, "No, no, no. You get extra credit if you make it to the rest room."

AMY VAN DYKEN
Olympic gold medalist in swimming

Winning is like shaving; you do it every day or you wind up looking like a bum.

JACK KEMP
Former NFL quarterback and U.S. congressman

To enhance my performance, I laugh a lot. I think laughter is the best remedy for everything.

———

TRICIA BYRNES

Halfpipe champion snowboarder in the 1999 World Cup

When I stood up there as a pinch hitter, I honestly believed I was the best hitter in the game. That's the only attitude to have.

MANNY MOTA
One of MLB's best pinch hitters

Have confidence in yourself and don't let people put you down or make you feel weak or worthless, because the more they put you down, the more you need to get back up and prove how wrong they are.

LAYNE BEACHLEY
World champion surfer

I have nothing to
prove to anyone.
I only play for myself.

MARK PHILIPPOUSSIS
Australian tennis star

My advice is that going to the Olympics and winning a gold medal are great goals, but the real goal should be to be the best that you can be.

DEBI THOMAS

World champion figure skater and medical doctor

You work your whole life
to try to be the best
you can, even if it's
for only one day or
one week.

LINDSAY DAVENPORT
Wimbledon champion

Confidence comes from hard work. It comes from facing different situations and making putts. It comes from knowing you've worked on the right things, so when you get under the gun, you can execute what you've practiced.

DAVID DUVAL

British Open champion

You can want it too much. You can try too hard. There's a point where you just have to let your muscle memory kick in.

CAROL HEISS JENKINS
1960 Olympic figure skating gold medalist

A winner's strongest muscle is her heart.

CASSIE CAMPBELL

*Gold medalist for Team Canada at the 1994 and 1997
Women's World Hockey Championships*

People don't win
because they're
physically stronger.
It's because they're
stronger between the ears.

———

ALEX SHAFFER
U.S. alpine skier

Being gifted intellectually is only a small part of the equation of success. Concentrate on the factors you have control over: persistence, self-discipline, confidence. Far more failures are due to lack of will than lack of ability.

TERRY BRADSHAW
Hall of Fame NFL quarterback

Never mistake activity for achievement.

BILL WALTON
Hall of Fame basketball player

You face adversity all the time. I accept what lies ahead and then I do my best. You can't take things too seriously, and you can't use things as an excuse or you'll never get through.

KRISTINE LILLY

World Cup star and winner of the Hermann Trophy, college soccer's highest honor

The ones who are successful are the ones who really want it. You have to have that inner drive otherwise it's not going to work out.

KERRI STRUG
Olympic gold medalist in gymnastics

You don't have to win to be a winner. If you give 100 percent, getting yourself mentally and physically prepared to play the game, if you look in the mirror and can say you gave it everything to win, that's it. You're not going to win every time.

———

DUKE SNIDER
Hall of Fame baseball player

Never look where you're going. Always look where you want to go.

BOB ERNST

Rowing coach at the University of Washington

You can have a certain
arrogance, and I think
that's fine. But what you
should never lose is the
respect for others.

STEFFI GRAF

Winner of all four tennis Grand Slams

All my life I've been
a late bloomer.
What's important is
just that you bloom.

CHIP BECK
PGA golfer

I want my life to be measured not by the pain and hardships I've endured, but by my will to keep moving forward, setting goals, working hard and seeking excellence.

DENNIS GREEN
Former NFL head coach

Everyone wants to win, but I think winners believe they deserve to win. They've made the commitment, they've followed the right path, and they've taken the right steps to be successful.

AMY RULEY

Basketball coach at North Dakota State University

Success is doing
what it takes
in spite of
one's fear.

JOHNNY RUTHERFORD

Three-time Indy 500 champion

Fear is okay.
Fear keeps you
on your toes.

ROBYN BENINCASA

She and her three male teammates won the
Eco-Challenge Sabah 2000 adventure race

As soon as you
start focusing on the
negative you're dead.

LIBBY HICKMAN

Member of the 2000 U.S. Olympic track team

I hate to lose more than
I like to win. I hate to
see the happiness on
their faces when they
beat me!

JIMMY CONNORS
Tennis star and winner of the U.S. Open

Winning is like a deodorant. It covers up a lot that stinks.

DOC RIVERS
Coach of the NBA Orlando Magic

Sometimes you're
the pigeon and
sometimes you're
the statue.

BERNIE BICKERSTAFF

Former head coach of the Washington Wizards

G od gave me this gift and he can take it away just as quick. I don't want to tempt him by not practicing. There's nothing I'd rather do than play golf.

LEE TREVINO
Winner of the U.S. and British Opens and
PGA Championship

I don't agree with the idea that you have to live in a bubble and sacrifice all your time to something if you want to succeed. I need to be interested in things outside my sport, and I need to meet new people. For me, judo is an expression of the harmony I achieve in my life.

RYOKO TAMURA

Four-time world judo champion and Olympic bantamweight silver medalist in 1992 and 1996, for Japan

I'll go out and do my best. I'm not afraid to fail. My father has a saying, "If you're worried, you're not praying," and I pray a lot.

———

SHAUN KING
NFL quarterback

I've found that staying relaxed makes me mentally tougher. So when the opportunity to win presents itself, I can allow myself to seize it.

MARK O'MEARA
Masters and British Open champion

If you try hard and you have fun and you're a good sport, you're a success no matter what the score or where you finish. You could be perfectly prepared. You could do absolutely everything right. You could run the best race of your life and other people could beat you. That doesn't mean you are not a success.

NANCY DITZ

Marathon runner ranked number one in the United States in 1987 and 1988

I didn't want to look back when I'm an old man and say, "You had a special talent and you didn't get the most of it." That's been a real motivating factor for me, something I think about every day.

KERRY COLLINS
New York Giants quarterback

Get out there and do your best and don't think!

JUDY RANKIN
U.S. Solheim Cup captain's advice to the U.S. team

When I'm out there I don't think. I don't fathom. I play. I never think, Wow. How did I make that throw? Nothing I have ever done has surprised me, because it's all within the realm of my ability.

KURT WARNER

Super Bowl MVP quarterback for the St. Louis Rams

Confidence is everything.
If you start second-
guessing yourself,
you're bound to run
into more bad outings.

————

TREVOR HOFFMAN
San Diego Padres relief pitcher

Only the strong survive.

JENNIFER CAPRIATI

Winner of the Australian and French Opens in 2001

Don't worry about people who are ahead of you or behind you. Your concentration has to be on what you're doing. Once you lose that concentration, that's when things go awry.

WALTER PAYTON
NFL Hall of Fame running back

Any team can be a miracle team. The catch is you have to work for a miracle. Effort is what separates journeyman players from impact players.

PAT RILEY
Head coach of the Miami Heat

I'm one of the leaders on the team, and I feel my attitude sets the tone. It's my job to magnify my teammates' strengths and hide their weaknesses. I put people in position to do their thing.

DAWN STALEY

Former point guard of the WNBA Charlotte Sting and now women's coach at Temple

It's a tough job to be back-up. You truly need to have a B team, and you need to make those team members feel they have a constructive role. You have to give them an honest assessment of what their chances are to make the A team. At the same time, you've got to give them their dream, their reason for doing it.

———

JJ ISLER

U.S. Olympic silver medalist in sailing and member of the America's Cup Mighty Mary

It's usually the guys who put up big numbers who get the credit, but the little guys put up the little numbers at crucial times.

BILL RUSSELL

Former MLB player and coach

When love and discipline come together you have great chemistry.

RICK PITTINO
Basketball coach at Louisville

L eadership is a matter of having people look at you and gain confidence, seeing how you react. If you're in control, they're in control.

TOM LANDRY
Former head coach of the Dallas Cowboys

The process of getting there—all the blood, sweat, and tears, all the lumps and disappointments—is what makes winning great. If you do something really, really hard, and you do it as a team effort, there is nothing like it in the world.

JOE GIBBS

Three-time Super Bowl–winning coach and owner of Joe Gibbs Racing (NASCAR)

Team chemistry is a trite phrase. It's overused. A team is judged on whether it is a winner or not. Winning is the bottom line.

———

GEORGE STEINBRENNER
Owner of the New York Yankees

I've learned that failure precedes success, and the right decisions are an extension of the wrong ones.

ALEX SPANOS
Owner of the San Diego Chargers

I don't work this hard just to be the best player. I do it to win.

HOLLY MCPEAK

Pro beach volleyball player

It's always about winning. Anybody who says it doesn't matter whether you win or lose is going to lose.

JOE MONTANA

Hall of Fame NFL quarterback

The cream always rises to the top. I'm a good example of that. Not exactly whipped cream. I'm kind of an ugly foam.

REX HUDLER
Former MLB utility player

Just because your muscles start to protest doesn't mean you have to listen.

DIANNE HOLUM

Winner of four Olympic medals, including a gold, in speed skating in two Olympics

The greatest lesson I learned in life is you have to appreciate the moments in your life that are hard. You can't run from adversity. You have to let it hit you straight in the face.

TRENT DILFER

NFL Super Bowl quarterback for the 2001 champion Baltimore Ravens

If you're not prepared, it's not pressure you feel, it's fear.

BRUCE BOCHY

Manager of the San Diego Padres

I have the strength, the ability of taking the pain. It's not like someone is forcing me to do it. I know that I will do my best. And I know that nothing comes without pain.

TEGLA LOROUPE

Kenyan Olympian who competed in both the marathon and the 10,000-meters in the Sydney Games

In the end, it is how we face challenge, how we strive to reach the goal that determines what kind of people we are.

JOHN THOMPSON

Former basketball coach at Georgetown University

The great athletes don't have to think about it. They just go out and do it. The ones who don't have as much ability have to convince themselves that they can play.

JIMMY CEFALO

Former wide receiver for the Miami Dolphins

I don't want to
look back—I want
to keep looking ahead.
I'd hate for my defining
moment to be my past.

SCOTT HAMILTON

Olympic gold medalist in figure skating

A real champion is somebody who can act like a gentleman and perform like a gentleman when things are not going well.

PETER JACOBSEN
PGA golfer

M ake it a point to be around those with positive energy—people who want what's best for you, people who understand your goals and priorities.

REBECCA LOBO

Female college basketball Player of the Year in 1995

If I don't do what I need to do to win, I won't win, no matter who is on the other side of the net.

ANDRE AGASSI

U.S., French, Australian, and Wimbledon champion

I train so hard to make sure failure doesn't happen. If I do everything I can, and run as fast as I possibly can and someone still beats me, I don't think of that as failure.

MARION JONES

*Winner of five Olympic medals in track and field
at the Sydney Games*

Everybody loves success,
but they hate
successful people.

JOHN MCENROE

U.S. Open tennis champion and TV analyst

Time has put racing in its place for me. If racing had been the only thing in my life, I wouldn't have been a very happy person. But I learned my family loved me whether I won or lost.

———

MICHAEL WALTRIP

2001 winner of the Daytona 500

Whatever you fear,
go there.

BILLIE JEAN KING

*Tennis great who was honored with the
Elizabeth Blackwell Award for her championing of
gender equity and her advocacy of women's rights*

Happiness is derived from achievement and achievement is derived from overcoming something that at first might have been difficult. Achievement is a valuable thing in our society and teaches you, as an athlete, that you can overcome fears and you can push through things that are uncomfortable.

MICHELE MITCHELL-ROCHA
Diving coach at the University of Arizona

In order to hit a good golf shot at that moment in time when you're standing over the ball, you must believe that golf shot is the most important thing in your life.

TIGER WOODS
Youngest winner of all four Grand Slam tournaments

The only person who can stop you from reaching your goals is you.

JACKIE JOYNER-KERSEE

World record holder in the heptathlon and winner of six Olympic gold medals

We have the misconception that competitiveness means winning at all costs, but that's not what competition is. Competition is just doing your best and not giving up. We all face a moment in a race or in a competition in which we want to give up. We can either give in and not keep pushing, or we can charge forward and work through it.

———

LISA RAINSBERGER
Winner of the Boston Marathon

Don't be afraid to win.

LARRY BROWN

Coach of the NBA Philadelphia 76ers

You've got to put those bad shots behind you. That's why some people win a lot more than others. They have the ability to forget about a bad swing and think about the good stuff.

LAURA DAVIES
LPGA golfer

I really don't have any long-term goals. For example, I don't say I want to be No. 1 in the world or anything like that. I just want to keep improving. So every three or four months for the last year and a half, I've stepped it up a level. I think if I can continue to do that, things should take care of themselves.

ANDY RODDICK
Member of the U.S. Davis Cup team

In life,
not just in sports,
if you don't try,
you cannot know
what you can do.

MANON RHEAUME

First woman to play in a National Hockey League game

If you aren't going all the way, why go at all?

JOE NAMATH

NFL Hall of Fame quarterback

I'm not afraid to take a step and if I fall, I fall. I pick myself up and move on. If we can all learn one thing in life, it's don't be afraid to take on something that you believe you're capable of achieving.

MICHAEL JORDAN
Basketball legend

It's easy to say success is having a gold medal or winning a championship, but I think it is much more than that. It's being able to know I did absolutely everything I could possibly do to win. The results are less significant than the effort.

KELLY WILLIAMS
U.S. Fencing Association's 1998 Female
Athlete of the Year

I always practice as I intend to play.

JACK NICKLAUS
One of golf's greatest players

My dad always felt if you worked really hard you would be a success, but I've learned that that approach is a strength *and* a weakness. It wasn't until I learned to let go a little bit that I became a top player. You know: Work hard, but when you play, *play.*

TOM KITE

U.S. Open golf champion

Everyone is really afraid of getting out there and not being good. That's the challenge: To be afraid and know people are staring at you and know you might not do all that well, but you do it anyway. What singles out the successful athlete from the ones who never make it past a plateau, is that successful athletes risk failure, even though they are terrified.

AIMEE MULLINS
Double-amputee track star

Anybody who plays sports and says they've never choked is lying to you.

PETE SAMPRAS
Seven-time Wimbledon champion

You have to chase your dreams, no matter what. The impossible just takes a little longer. One stroke at a time, one step at a time, the impossible is easy to achieve.

TORI MURDEN
First woman to row across the Atlantic Ocean alone

You accomplish victory
step by step,
not by leaps and bounds.

LYN ST. JAMES
Indy race car driver

I'm very much a goal-oriented person. I set a goal for every shot to each nine holes, to the eighteenth hole, to seventy-two holes, to the day, to the week, to the month, to the year.

GREG NORMAN
International Golf Hall of Fame member

Have fun,
always set goals
but never set limits.

SHANNON MILLER

Olympic gold medalist in gymnastics

A top athlete has to combine three different factors: physical strength, tactics, and mental toughness. The golden rule is to never let any of those slip.

FELICIA BALLANGER

Ten-time cycling gold medalist at world championships and gold medalist for France in match sprint at the 1996 Olympics

Y ou must play to your strengths and downplay your weaknesses. The world is full of people who dramatically turned their lives around, merely by recognizing their own strengths and going with them.

BRUCE JENNER
Olympic gold medalist in decathalon

I kept myself calm
by making sure I didn't
concentrate on anything
I couldn't control.

B. J. BEDFORD

U.S. Olympic swimmer in 2000

I don't know anybody who knows how to get into the zone. It's more of how do you remove the barriers that keep you out of the zone.

NANCY HALLER
Sports psychologist

All progress requires change. But not all change is progress.

JOHN WOODEN
Hall of Fame college basketball coach and player

A lot of people notice
when you succeed,
but they don't see what
it takes to get there.

———————

DAWN STALEY
Olympic basketball star

I've gotten a long way just on sheer optimism— taking jobs I was unqualified for, never believing I would fail at them because I'm optimistic to the point of being naïve. I was willing to try things I probably should have failed at and could have failed at but didn't.

LIZ DOLAN

Former Nike executive and host of Satellite Sisters
on National Public Radio

I've learned not to listen to people who say I can't do things. If you have heart and determination, anything is possible.

BRIAN SHAY

All-time leading rusher in Division II college football, Emporia State, Kansas

You can accomplish so much with a strong will. Just do your best. No matter what. Don't let negative thoughts creep in. Don't talk yourself out of anything.

REBECCA TWIGG

Olympic cyclist, winner of a silver medal in 1984 and a bronze in 1992

You need your opponent to play. One of the things my coach taught me is this kid right across from you, he wants to win as much as you do. You need him. He's testing you. You're going to test him.

THOMAS TUTKO

Professor of sports psychology at San Jose State

You've got to look
for tough competition.
You've got to want
to beat the best.

GRETE WAITZ
Winner of a record nine New York City Marathons

Talent only gives you the opportunity to win.

CHAD BROWN
Seattle Seahawks linebacker

I don't want to lose my intensity. You shouldn't let your emotions get the best of you, but I also like to keep my edge.

PIERRE PAGE
NHL head coach

There were times when deep down inside I wanted to win so badly I could actually will it to happen. I think most of my career was based on desire.

———

CHRIS EVERT
Winner of eighteen Grand Slam singles titles

Football doesn't build character, it reveals character.

MARV LEVY

Former NFL head coach

S wimming is a gift—my gift. It can't be about, "Kill the competitor." It's got to be about the gratification of achieving and making the most of it while I'm still physically able. Above all else, it's got to be about having the most fun that I can. Because that's when I truly feel like me.

JENNY THOMPSON

Olympic swimmer with seven gold medals

A pitcher never gets me out. I get myself out. That's no disrespect to the pitcher, but there should be no excuse for failure. You can't have an excuse to fail.

MIKE PIAZZA
All-star catcher for the New York Mets

Those who truly have the spirit of champions are never wholly happy with an easy win. Half the satisfaction stems from knowing it was the time and the effort you invested that led to your high achievement.

NICOLE HAISLETT
Olympic swimming champion

P atience? Who wants to hear that word? I'll tell you this. If the only thing you think about is the future, it's going to be somebody else's.

JIMMY JOHNSON
Former college and NFL head coach

I always believe I can beat the best, achieve the best. I always see myself in the top position.

SERENA WILLIAMS
1999 Women's U.S. Open tennis champion

There are so many people out there who will tell you that you can't. What you've got to do is turn around and say, "I can. Watch me."

LAYNE BEACHLEY
World champion surfer

You can get paralysis through analysis. You can concede to an opponent something he hasn't earned. It's one thing to underestimate an opponent. But maybe the worst thing is to overestimate. You always play to your strengths. But that doesn't mean you become predictable.

CHUCK KNOX
Former NFL head coach

Overthinking is often the problem in golf. Winning requires some forgetfulness. Suppress negative emotions. Concentration, composure, confidence. Just look and swing!

DR. NATE ZINSSER

Director of applied sports psychology at West Point

I believe stress keeps you from greatness. Creating all these weird distractions and concerns prevents you from examining your life and connecting with those parts of yourself that help you do bigger things.

———

GABRIELLE REECE
Pro beach volleyball player

When I was feeling pressure I'd tell myself that as long as I was a good sport, my mom would still love me.

MATT BIONDI

Winner of eleven Olympic medals in swimming, eight of them gold

We strive for excellence, both academically and athletically because the journey, the striving, is as pleasurable and important as the goal.

———

JOHN THOMPSON

Former basketball coach at Georgetown University

My three keys to success: One, work hard. Two, be your own person. And three, have a passion for what you're doing.

___

JULI INKSTER
LPGA Hall of Fame member

Ego is the drug
of stupidity.

DR. TOM AMBERRY
"The world's greatest free-throw shooter,"
according to The Guinness Book of World Records

I t's easy to get diverted by all the variables outside
your control, to let them eat away at your vision and
self-confidence. But detours will doom you. Lose faith in
yourself and you'll fulfill your worst prophecy.

BILL PARCELLS
Former NFL head coach

I just took on a new attitude: I'm going to go for it. I'm going to get the job done. I'm not going to hold back.

VENUS WILLIAMS

U.S. Open and Wimbledon champion

When you analyze any player—the more successful the player the more it's true—you'll find he has to be right about everything. If he doesn't have that ability, which is also a refusal to acknowledge he could be wrong, then he doesn't have the ability to pull a five-iron instead of a six when he has the choice. A player has to know that whatever he decides, he's right.

DEANE BEMAN
Former PGA Tour commissioner

All you can do is your best. You give it everything you have and whether you make it or not, you've done all you can. If you've done that, there's nothing else you can give and you should be proud of yourself.

JOY FAWCETT

Star player on the U.S. women's national soccer team and the WUSA Spirit

Motivation comes from within each individual. It's a personal thing. It's pride, guts, desire, whatever you want to call it; some people have it in their bellies, and some don't.

MIKE DITKA
Former NFL head coach

I train harder than anyone else in the world. Last year I was supposed to take a month off and I took three days off because I was afraid somebody out there was training harder. That's the feeling I go through every day— Am I not doing what somebody else is doing? Is someone out there training harder than I am? I can't live with myself if someone is.

MARION JONES
World-class sprinter and long jumper

S uccess is one of the biggest preventers of growth. People think, "Don't screw it up." So they don't change, and somebody else leaps ahead of them.

———

DOUG HALL
Author of Jump Start Your Brain

A champion is afraid
of losing. Everyone else
is afraid of winning.

BILLIE JEAN KING

Holder of a record twenty Wimbledon tennis titles

Pressure is a word that is misused in our vocabulary. When you start thinking of pressure, it's because you've started to think of failure.

TOMMY LASORDA

Former manager of the L.A. Dodgers and
2000 U.S. Olympic baseball team

It's okay to be scared, but don't let it dictate your actions.

MICHELE AKERS

Member of the U.S. women's national soccer team and only woman to win FIFA's highest honor, the Order of Merit

You can't measure success if you have never failed.

STEFFI GRAF

Winner of 22 Grand Slam tennis titles

I get over bad games right away. Sometimes I've let it go even before I've left the mound. That quick. Why? Because it's over. What can you do about it? Nothing. The only thing you can do is fight if you're still in the game. After that you can do nothing.

MARIANO RIIVERA
Star relief pitcher for the New York Yankees

I try not to get too caught up thinking about the task ahead. I just do what has to be done. I have the belief in myself that what I'm doing is right. Then I let the rest happen.

EAMONN COGHLAN

Former world record-holder in the indoor mile and the first masters runner to break the four-minute mile

I t's always better to focus on what to do now and not worry about what's going to happen later. If you're in the middle of a race, you shouldn't be thinking, "I hope I don't die in the last mile." You worry about the last mile when you get to it.

———

NANCY RIEDEL

Track and cross-country coach at Mira Costa College

You wake up today, you enjoy today. You have no control of tomorrow and you've lost control of yesterday. You go inning by inning.

JOE TORRE
New York Yankees manager talking about life after cancer surgery

One thing we always talk about around here is that it ain't where you start out but where you finish. Make sure your last game is your best game, because you always remember that one.

———

NATE NEWTON
Dallas Cowboys offensive guard

There's a fine line between being conceited and having confidence in yourself. Conceit is thinking you can do it without hard work and perseverance.

CAROL HEISS JENKINS
Olympic gold medalist in figure skating

Great players never look in the mirror and think, I'm a great basketball player. They ask themselves, "Am I the best player I can be?"

MICHAEL JORDAN
Hall of Fame basketball great

I love pushing my body to the limit and seeing how far I can take it before it breaks.

AMY VAN DYKEN

Olympic gold medalist in swimming

In order to be the best,
you have to know
your breaking point—
go to the edge of it,
but never go beyond.

REBECCA TWIGG

Olympic cyclist

You can never turn
a switch on and off.
It's got to always be on.

TIGER WOODS

Number-one-ranked golfer in the world

The harder you work, the harder it is to surrender.

PAT SUMMITT
Women's basketball coach at Tennessee,
six-time national champions

Stubbornness is a
virtue if you're right.
It's only a character flaw
if you're wrong.

———

CHUCK NOLL

Former NFL head coach, Pittsburgh Steelers

S ometimes you have to let events unfold in front of you, and attack when the opportunities are there. It's hard to accept that some things are not in your control.

NOTAH BEGAY III
PGA golfer

People do their best
work when they just
let go. I learned that
in gymnastics.

CATHY RIGBY

First U.S. gymnast to medal in world-class competition
and star of the stage musical Peter Pan

The most exciting thing in a tournament is to be in the hunt. Your heart is pumping so fast. You get into your own little world. I don't really pay any attention to my opponent. It's just a matter of doing my work.

ANNIKA SORENSTAM
2001 LPGA Player of the Year

S ometimes trying harder is worse than being relaxed. We're loose. We play music, laugh, and joke around. That's what makes it so exciting to come to the ballpark, that Little League attitude. Sleep in your uniform, come to the ballpark, swing from your heels, and try to hit homers.

———

JASON GIAMBI
MLB all-star first baseman

The best teams try
to fix things when
they're winning, not
after they start to lose.

KEVIN CONSTANTINE

NHL coach

I love to compete and I love to run, but if I boil all my self-worth and my entire athletic career to losing a race, I can't deal with it. You can't motivate yourself to get out there and do it again if you focus on one devastating race. So instead, I concentrate on my own personal goals.

LISA RAINSBERGER
Winner of the Boston Marathon

You can't be afraid to try things in life. Set your goals high, and you'll get at least a part of the way there.

DAWN RILEY

Skipper of America True syndicate in America's Cup sailing competition

I never set out to
beat the world. I just
set out to do my
absolute best.

AL OERTER

Winner of four Olympic gold medals in the discus

First of all you need to find what you are interested in—what you enjoy doing. Then pursue that avenue and its opportunities. Once you do that you start realizing your potential and what you can accomplish. That's when you set your goals. I believe in setting goals and trying to reach them.

_____

SUZIE MCCONNELL SERIO
Olympic and WNBA star

Life isn't about what will make you rich; it's about what will enrich you.

DR. LA MAR HASBROOK
Former football player at UC Berkeley who is now a medical doctor

Believing in yourself is everything. If you don't believe in what you can do, it's almost impossible to achieve it.

SYLVIE BERNIER

Canadian Olympic gold medalist in diving in 1984

The most important thing is to love your sport. Never do it to please someone else—it has to be yours. That is all that will justify the hard work needed to achieve success. Compete against yourself, not others, for that is who is truly your best competition.

PEGGY FLEMING

Figure skating gold medalist in the 1968 Winter Olympics

You have to follow your heart. If you can't give something all of your heart you shouldn't do it.

SHANE WALTON

Notre Dame football player and former soccer star

L ife is a journey, and you are a fool if you experience it with just your body. You have to live it through your mind and heart.

JIM BROWN
NFL Hall of Fame running back

My parents always told us to find out what we were good at and not worry about what others think.

LORNAH KIPLAGAT

Kenyan runner who was the first woman in twenty-eight years to win both the Peachtree Road Race and the Falmouth Road Race in the same year (2000)

If you don't think like a winner, you're not going to be a winner.

ZAK KUSTOK

Former quarterback at Northwestern University

There are certain times when you work, work, work, practice, practice, practice, and the physical part's there but emotionally something's happening in your life or mentally you're a little slack. It's very rare when all three—the physical, the mental, and the emotional—come together. I think what makes a champion is when one thing's on but two things are off, and you still win the match.

CHRIS EVERT

First sixteen-year-old to be a U.S. Open tennis semifinalist

One day I had an epiphany. I said to myself, "Yes, I am different, but instead of that being a bad thing, I can have the best of two worlds." I learned to love to be unique.

SHANE BATTIER

Duke basketball All-American and winner of the John Wooden Award

It was only after I changed my belief from an external focus—beating others—to an internal focus that my behavior could change. My new belief said that my self-worth was based on doing my best.

HENRY MARSH

Competed on four U.S. Olympic track and field teams;
America's best steeplechaser

You've got to race for yourself. You've got to find something in your efforts that has meaning to you, and only you can define that. Once you define it, you are going to be much more at peace with what you are doing.

SILKEN LAUMANN
Canadian Olympic medalist in rowing

The great player, when he has his off day, shoots a better score. He never knuckles under. He goes with the flow, never quits, understands there are going to be mistakes, and battles, battles, battles.

ROGER MALTBIE
TV analyst and Senior PGA tour player

The victory wasn't in winning (which we ended up doing), it was in totally swimming our hearts out and being able to celebrate the fact that we had our best possible swim and entertained the people watching, regardless of where we placed.

CLAIRE CARVER-DIAS

Canadian Olympic synchronized swimmer describing
her team's victory at the Pan Am Games

Y ou have people telling you how good you are and all of a sudden, you might start believing it and forget what it takes to be good.

LOU LAMORIELLO
NHL Devils general manager

You can never meet
everyone's expectations.
It's hard enough to
meet your own.

ANDREA JAEGER

Won her first professional tennis tournament when she
was only fourteen years old

The one strongest, most important part of my game is that I want to be the best. I won't accept anything less than that. My ability to concentrate and work toward that goal has been my greatest asset.

JACK NICKLAUS
Winner of 18 major golf chamionships

A true champion works
hard and never loses
sight of her dreams.

DOT RICHARDSON

Olympic gold medalist in softball, and orthopedic surgeon

I love to make mistakes.
I've made more
mistakes than I've done
things right. But then
they're gone. Over.

SPARKY ANDERSON

*Former manager of the Cincinnati Reds
and the Detroit Tigers*

Success starts with the fact that you have to live with integrity. If you don't have integrity, you get lost.

STEVE YOUNG

*Former Super Bowl–winning quarterback
of the San Francisco 49ers*

The medals don't mean anything and the glory doesn't last. It's all about your happiness. The rewards are going to come, but the happiness is just loving the sport and having fun performing.

JACKIE JOYNER-KERSEE

World record holder in the heptathlon and winner of six Olympic gold medals

You don't have to be number one to be a winner. Being a winner is going out and doing everything you can to do your best, but also being gracious when you come out on top and gracious when you don't.

DEBI THOMAS
World and national champion in figure skating

You have to think your way through the challenges you're presented with. You have to exploit vulnerability, but you can't if you don't know what it is you're trying to exploit. Thinking encompasses seeing, reading, anticipating the play, and understanding strengths, yours and your opponents'.

CRAIG BUTTON
NHL Calgary Flames general manager

I just never give up. I fight till the end. I can't accept not fighting. You can't go out and say, "I want a bag of never-say-die spirit." It's not for sale. It has to be innate.

SERENA WILLIAMS
U.S. Open tennis champion

You've got to
accomplish something
to have confidence.
Winning helps.

BERNIE BICKERSTAFF

Former NBA coach

When they say golf is 90 percent mental, they're really talking about attitude. The right attitude is the first step of playing your best.

————

WENDY WARD
Golf Digest *playing editor*

A losing football team looks at excuses. A championship football team looks at solutions.

JIMMY JOHNSON

Former Dallas Cowboys and Miami Dolphins head coach

I used to be the sorest loser, but I've learned that kind of attitude prevents you from getting anything out of a defeat.

HILLARY WOLF
Member of the 2000 Olympic judo team

To be the very best you can be, you have to have the intellect. My body just does what my mind tells it to. Losers quit. When you have a sound mind, you can do what's necessary.

EVANDER HOLYFIELD
Heavyweight boxing champion

Success is setting goals for yourself and achieving them. Never compare your successes with other people's successes because that's not what it's about. It's about your own goals, writing them down on a piece of paper and then achieving them. Don't worry about what everyone else is doing.

CASSIE CAMPBELL
Olympic hockey player for Team Canada

Somewhere
along the line,
   people motivated
only by money
   lose the edge.

JEREMY MCGRATH

*All-time leader in Supercross wins
and season championships*

Either you have your dreams or you live your dreams. I'm not all that remarkable. I just keep putting one foot in front of the other until I get to where I have to go. Everybody's got their finish line in life. This is mine. People need to know that success isn't all about winning.

ZOE KOPLOWITZ

Suffering from multiple sclerosis, she walked the New York City Marathon in twenty-eight hours, with the aid of two custom-made canes

You've got to think you can win, no matter what age you are.

ARNOLD PALMER
Hall of Fame golf legend

I think success is how you conduct your life, not just if you win games. I want to be great at what I do, but I care how I do it. I don't want to cheat somebody for a win. I don't want to lie to somebody for a job. Success to me is how you handle yourself day in and day out. Success is consistency.

NANCY LIEBERMAN-CLINE
TV basketball analyst and former WNBA head coach

I'm into the process of winning, not just winning. People who worry just about winning don't always win.

PIERRE PAGE
NHL head coach

People get paralyzed when they become really successful because they start thinking, "I don't want to fail." You have to keep attacking, putting yourself in situations where you could possibly fail. You have to stick your neck out where you could take a fall.

GABRIELLE REECE
Beach volleyball star, TV host, and author

To win you must have talent and desire—but desire is first.

SAM SNEAD
Hall of Fame golfer

The ultimate rare athlete is the one who will actually play for the joy of the competition and has no fear. Most people play with fear. Fear in life, fear in their participation in athletics. It's, "I hope I don't look bad, I hope I don't choke, I hope I can do it." It's almost like they want to win but there's too much fear there.

JOHNNY MILLER

U.S. Open champion and TV golf analyst

Two things help me be a winner. One is I try to stay on an even keel. I don't get too high or too low. Two is I do a lot of visualization. I never see a bad pitch. I always see a good one.

ILA BORDERS

First woman to ever be a starting pitcher in a men's professional baseball game

Chance favors the prepared mind.

CHUCK KNOX
Former NFL head coach

Getting in that ring, I experienced something that most people on the planet have not experienced. I was totally enlightened. That ability to program pain out of your being for a few rounds is an amazing thing. It shows what you can do as a human being.

ALICIA DOYLE
Professional boxer

Don't rate potential over performance.

HAL SHERBECK

Former football coach at Fullerton College

I think of myself as an eternal optimist. All I need is one shred of evidence and I go crazy. It's not reality that's important, it's what we think we are.

SHELLY HAMLIN
1992 LPGA Bounceback Player of the Year

You can't worry about what somebody else is doing. You come out and work hard every day. You play and let your performance speak for you. If things don't work out, at least you know you gave it everything you had.

CLIF GROCE

Former running back for the Indianapolis Colts

N ever ask for victory, ask only for courage. For if you endure the struggle, you bring honor to yourself. But more important, you bring honor to us all.

BILL MALLON
Author of Quest for Gold:
The Encyclopedia of American Olympians

I made my disappointment a motivation, and it paid off. I wouldn't have gotten a medal four years ago, so not making the team has given me four years of motivation.

MARI HOLDEN

U.S. Olympic cyclist who won the silver medal in the women's time trial at the 2000 Olympics talking about being left off the 1996 team after winning the Olympic Trials

People fall down.
Winners get up.
Gold medal winners
get up the fastest.

BONNIE ST. JOHN

Paralympic medal–winning skier and Rhodes scholar

I dentify your personal limits, and then push past them. Then set new barriers, and repeat the process, again and again and again.

NICOLE HAISLETT

Winner of three gold medals in swimming in the 1992 Olympic Games

You expect success,
you respect failure.

GREG NORMAN
Two-time British Open champion

Sports taught me that I can make a mistake one minute, let it go, and be brilliant the next.

LYNN SHERR

Correspondent for ABC's 20/20

S ure you blew it tonight, but when it's over, it's over. Let it go. Otherwise you won't be ready to play tomorrow night.

DAVE DEBUSSCHERE
Former NBA star of the New York Knicks

We were in the bathroom, in the mirror, all the athletes. We were putting on makeup. And we just started laughing. It's a performance when you go out there and run. If you look good, you feel good. And when you feel good, you race good.

SHARON COUCH

U.S. Olympic hurdler describing her experience at the 1992 Barcelona Olympics

Everyone has some fear.
A man who has no fear
belongs in a
mental institution.
Or on special teams.

WALT MICHAELS
Former New York Jets head coach

You have to remember that no matter how big your goals or how many you have, there are going to be times when you miss by a little bit. You have to be realistic and flexible. One reason I have so many smaller goals is that even if my big goals don't happen, I've still achieved so much along the way, I don't feel the loss.

SHANNON MILLER

The most decorated gymnast in U.S. history with seven Olympic and nine World Championship medals

You get into the feeling like you are in a zone. You can't be stopped. It's a good feeling but it never lasts. People catch up to you, and that's when you have to do something different.

DAN MARINO
Hall of Fame NFL quarterback

S uccess is aiming for the stars, because if you fall
 short, you're going to land on the moon, and there
are not too many people on the moon now, are there?

———

AMY VAN DYKEN

First American woman to win four gold medals in a
single Olympics (swimming in 1996)

I don't know that it's true that you learn more from losing than from winning. I do know that you improve a lot more if you win.

ROD LAVER

Only two-time winner of the Grand Slam in tennis

If a team wants to intimidate you physically and you let them, they've won.

MIA HAMM

Member of the U.S. national soccer team,
1999 World Cup champions

When the race is over, if you know a sleepless night helped you work harder to do better the next day, then you did your best.

PAUL O'NEIL

Retired New York Yankee with five World Series rings

I t's a small window, when you have really good players, to do something great. When you take a person and put him in a situation where he is having fun, his possibilities are limitless.

MARSHALL FAULK
MVP running back for the NFL St. Louis Rams

I just made a decision that I was going to make this team. I was expecting that from me. I wasn't going to use an injury or anything else as an excuse. It was my responsibility, and I wanted it so bad, I had to make it happen.

MARLA RUNYON

U.S. Olympic runner in the 1500-meters who competed in the 2000 Sydney Games and suffers from Stargardt's disease, a degenerative condition that began eroding her eyesight when she was nine

I compete because I love to compete. I love to win but there's a bigger picture. I go out and give it my best.

RICK DRANEY

One of the world's top-ranked wheelchair tennis players

Sometimes we get
so afraid of hitting bad
shots, we don't let
ourselves hit good ones.

———

BUTCH HARMON
Renowned golf instructor

Our goal going into the season is to win the World Series. Our goal isn't, "Let's make the playoffs this year, or let's win the AL pennant." If we don't win the World Series, then the season is a failure.

―――――――

DEREK JETER
New York Yankees star shortstop

I n sports, the more you can stay inside yourself the more chance you have to win or to be successful. As soon as you start dealing with the player on the other side of the net, you've got a big problem.

AHMAD RASHAD
Former NFL wide receiver and avid tennis player

Everybody has some nagging injury. We decided not to complain about them because what are you going to do? You've got to suck it up and play. And we didn't come here just to play, we came here to win a medal.

———

DANIELLE SCOTT
U.S. Olympic volleyball player

We are not going to lose because of the pressure. If we lose, it's because the other team just outplayed us, and that's been our philosophy all year.

LOU PINIELLA

Manager of the Seattle Mariners

When you're under siege, it's important to maintain your values, when it's easy to say, "To hell with it." There's always going to be change in this business. There are no guarantees that working long hours translates into wins.

TED TOLLNER

Former head football coach at USC and San Diego State

I wasn't handed a spot on the Olympic team. I've never been the type of player who was given anything. I had to earn my way back, and that couldn't be taken for granted.

TERESA EDWARDS
Olympic basketball star who played in a record five Olympics

Normally, when you win a big match, your coach and your parents are happy. It's different when you're playing for your country. It makes it a little more emotional. There was no reason to hide what I was feeling.

ANDY RODDICK

On winning a Davis Cup match to clinch a U.S. team victory against India

Having your sport in the Olympics raises the whole level of competition. You make sacrifices you wouldn't make in everyday life to get to the Olympics. I love art, I love going out with friends and to the movies. I've had to cut a lot of that out. I still haven't taken my honeymoon. But now I know what it takes to be an athlete at a high level. I can appreciate the effort of these athletes, whether they are in first place or last.

JENNIFER GUTIERREZ
U.S. Olympic triathlete

The possibility of losing
never enters your mind.
At least not in any of
the good players that
I know.

TED SCHROEDER
Wimbledon champion

W hen you're out on the water training for hours, striving for the perfect stroke, it's easy to lash out. You have to let the little stuff go and think about the bigger cause.

SARAH GARNER

1998 world champion rower talking about the relationship with her pairs partner

Life for me is about challenges and opportunity, and I intend to climb another mountain. A lot has happened in my life for the past thirty years, but the challenge is more important than what the past has meant.

MIKE DITKA

Former NFL head coach

I f I listened to my critics, I would have stopped jumping. But I listen to what my heart says and what my mind says. I don't think I could live with myself if I didn't try.

MARION JONES
Winner of five Olympic medals including the bronze medal in the long jump at the Sydney Games

W hat we tried to do is say, "Players are going to make mistakes, but it's a players' game." Our job isn't to micromanage every decision they make. Because then players become afraid to make mistakes. And when you get players who are inhibited or fear being criticized, then you don't have a very healthy environment.

APRIL HEINRICHS
Coach of the U.S. women's national soccer team

Look at all the positives and negatives of any situation, and then go back to one thing— what your heart tells you.

CHRIS WEINKE
Heisman Trophy winner

We kept believing in ourselves, and everyone went up to the plate believing they were going to get a hit. We just battled all the way. It was incredible. We persevered and dug deep. You can tell a champion by how she handles adversity and we sure had plenty of adversity.

MICHELE SMITH

U.S. Olympic softball pitcher talking about how the 2000 team came back to win the gold medal after losing three straight games

Thinking too much
about how you're doing
when you're doing
is disastrous.

HARVEY PENICK

Famous golf teacher

I don't think luck is involved in track and field. Skill dictates what happens. When someone says, "Good luck," I tell them, "I don't need good luck, I need all my skill."

GAIL DEVERS
Winner of two Olympic gold medals in the 100-meters

It's easy to stand back, but to move forward and take a chance, that takes a little more guts, a little more courage.

VENUS WILLIAMS
Wimbledon and U.S. Open champion

I love the competitive spirit. I don't play golf to be the number one in the world. I play it to be the best I can be every time I perform on the golf course. Sometimes it's good. Sometimes it's bad. You have to take the good with the bad. We're only human beings. We're going to make screw-ups, we're going to make good things out of bad things and bad things out of good things.

GREG NORMAN
Member of the International Golf Hall of Fame

This wasn't exactly what they thought nuns were cut out to do. But that didn't keep me from realizing we don't need to apologize for the gifts God gave us. But we do need to use them for his greater glory.

SISTER MADONNA BUDER

Seventy-year-old triathlete who holds both the 60–64 and the 65–69 age group records in the Ironman Triathlon World Championship

When it's getting late in a close game, those are the times I'm most relaxed. I don't think about the situation directly, but I'm aware of what's going on. I can feel myself getting looser. It's like I'm in my element.

———

CHRIS DRURY
NHL Colorado Avalanche center

The rewards for those who persevere far exceed the pain that precedes the victory.

KAREN BLISS LIVINGSTON

Elite road racer, captain of the Saturn cycling team

The game is played with the heart. You don't have to drink or swear or hit people in the face when they're not looking, but you do have to be tough to win.

TOM LANDRY

Former head coach of the Dallas Cowboys

Being a champion in life
is more important than
a gold medal.
That stays with you
forever.

———

ESTHER KIM
Tae kwon do champion

W e're not going to take votes. I'm going to give you a real clear picture of where this boat is going. What I expect from you is to get on board, put your oars in the water, and start rowing.

RANDY WALKER

Head football coach at Northwestern University

The sickness I feel when we lose is a lot more intense than the exhilaration I feel in victory. However, I pay the price. A lot of people want to achieve success, but only a few are willing to pay the price.

VIVIAN STRINGER
Rutgers University women's basketball coach

If you think about
what's on the line and
take the weight of it out
to the mound with you,
you can't perform.

MIKE MUSSINA
New York Yankee pitcher

The important thing to remember is, when you're told by your coach to sit on the bench, that's what you need to do, go sit on the bench. Then you need to make yourself useful.

———

JJ ISLER
Four-time Rolex Yachtswoman of the Year

The thing is,
    you have to engage
with life to have a life.

FRANK DEFORD

Renowned sportswriter and commentator

D on't make decisions because they are the easiest, the cheapest, or the most popular. Make your decision because it's right.

REV. THEODORE HESBURGH

Former president of Notre Dame

I don't want to look back on my life and say, "What if?" Don't worry about failure. Try it, and if it doesn't work out that's okay, because at least you tried.

ANNIE MEYERS DRYSDALE

First woman to be given a full athletic scholarship at UCLA and a member of the Basketball Hall of Fame

It's almost like you're born with it or you're not, and that's why certain people end up where they are and other people just wish they could. As time evolves, you just realize that you're a leader. If you recognize it, you want to make a conscious effort to use it in the best way possible. To me it's an ongoing process and a full-time job.

BRETT FAVRE
Quarterback of the Green Bay Packers

W inning championships isn't about being the best team. It's about getting bounces, working hard, and making things happen.

GREG VANNEY

Los Angeles Galaxy soccer player

Golf is less mind control and more emotional control. It is really important to concentrate solely on what you're doing at the present moment and not to think about winning or losing.

JUDY RANKIN
Winner of twenty-six LPGA tournaments

You want intelligent people, that's what we go after. Only sometimes the screwballs are first-teamers and the right guys are second-teamers. Some screwballs will win for you. You just want to have enough right guys to keep the screwballs under control.

JIMMY JOHNSON
Former NFL head coach and TV analyst

I'm so proud to be on this team. These guys make you want to be better, not just a better soccer player but a better person. When it's all said and done, that's the most important thing.

MIA HAMM

World Cup and Olympic soccer team member considered one of the greatest players ever

I told them you're playing for the name on the front of your uniform, not the one on the back. Of course, you have to believe you're the best player in the world as well, just don't tell anyone about it.

———

TOMMY LASORDA
His advice to his Japanese baseball team,
the 2001 Osaka Kintetsu Buffaloes

Liking what you do is hugely important. It gives you an extra drive that separates you from being just mediocre and makes you excel.

CLAIRE CARVER-DIAS
Member of Canada's 2000 Olympic synchronized swimming team

Perseverance is how most things get done and deals get made, because eventually, most of the world will just give up.

ROBERT KRAFT

Owner of the NFL New England Patriots,
2002 Super Bowl champions

You've always got to be aware of why you don't win, otherwise you'll keep losing. Every mistake is a learning experience and, hopefully, you won't make the same mistake again.

———

LAYNE BEACHLEY
World surfing champion

There's winning, and there's everything else.

STEVE YZERMAN
Canadian Olympic hockey player

I'm not exceptionally fast or overly powerful. But I have a good work ethic, and I make up for it by using technique and trying to be smarter.

DOT RICHARDSON

U.S. Olympic softball player on the 1996 and 2000 gold-medal-winning teams

I t's tough being number one with everyone expecting you to go out there and win. It's a great ride to get there, but then suddenly something mentally changes when you get there and you're playing as number one.

———

LINDSAY DAVENPORT
Wimbledon champion

When you win one, you want more. To me, four's not enough. So I'll celebrate this tonight and tomorrow and then in a week or two I'll start planning on how I can get another ring.

JEFF AGOOS

San Jose Earthquake defender after winning his
fourth MLS championship in 2001

There's a hell of a difference between doing it almost right and doing it right. The outcome of games, I think, are far more a result of mistakes than great plays.

BOBBY KNIGHT
Basketball coach of Texas Tech

The ideal way to win a championship is step by step. You're building, always building. Last year we never took any shortcuts, and we got there eventually.

PHIL JACKSON
Coach of the Los Angeles Lakers, back-to-back
NBA champions

P ressure doesn't bother me. My sister and I are the same way. Our mom and dad always told us that, no matter what happens, they were still going to love us. So there's no pressure. Just go out and play.

CHRIS LEWIS

*Stanford University quarterback whose sister
plays on the Stanford volleyball team*

One thing that was always valued in my family was being a whole person—spiritually, physically, and mentally. From that, I thought, Yeah, I can do all those things.

AMY ROSS

National champion 800-meter runner who is an army reservist on active duty and attends medical school

His secret is that he
attacks every drill,
he doesn't want to lose
at anything.

RICHARD HAMILTON

Washington Wizards player talking about Michael Jordan

You have to compete every day of your life, in everything. You compete if you're sick, if you're injured, if you don't feel like playing. It doesn't matter.

LLOYD CARR

Head football coach of the University of Michigan

The bigger the game
the better. I'm an
adrenaline junkie.
I feed off big crowds
and noise.

CURT SCHILLING

Arizona Diamondbacks pitcher, 2001 World Series co-MVP

I love playing tennis, I love winning titles. But I realized I wouldn't be any happier in my life in general if I won or lost. Sure, in the tennis part of my life I'd be much happier. But winning, losing, money, riches or fame doesn't make you happy. For my tennis career, this is great. But as far as being Venus, it doesn't really make a huge difference.

VENUS WILLIAMS
Top-ranked women's tennis player in the world

You need to have your convictions. You can't get away from the basics. Many times you get away from what you know—that's when you don't do well.

DON SHULA
Former head coach of the Miami Dolphins

W hat I represent is just achieving what you want to do in life. It's a matter of your attitude. Some people have a negative attitude, and that's their disability.

MARLA RUNYON
U.S. Olympic runner who is legally blind

I understand what it takes to be a champion. I told my players there is a price to pay for it—work, be in perfect condition and help their teammates by being team players.

LARRY BIRD

Hall of Fame basketball player and former head coach of the Indiana Pacers

If you trust your nerve
as well as your skill,
you're capable of
a lot more than you
can imagine.

DEBI THOMAS

World champion figure skater

W e're always working on something new, trying to get better. Knowing that you never arrive is a wonderful thing because you never say, "This is my limit."

TIGER WOODS

The world's number one golfer, talking about his work with coach Butch Harmon

I'm not a big stat guy. I definitely respect what those players did. I've always admired them. But I'm trying to focus on what I need to do. Stats are good to hear about and stuff, but they really don't help me put balls in the court. I'm not motivated by stats.

ANDY RODDICK
Member of the U.S. Davis Cup team

I was nervous but I heard this voice in my head just telling me, "Do what I know. Do what I know." As long as I did that, I'd be fine.

CATHY FREEMAN

Australian Olympic gold medalist in the 400-meters at the 2000 Olympics

People who can't handle pressure sense that times speeds up. Things happen more quickly for them, so they forget to do things. Those who can handle pressure find that their sense of time slows down.

PETER KOSTIS
PGA teaching professional and TV golf analyst

Ultimately, success is not measured by first place prizes. It's measured by the road we have traveled, how you dealt with the challenges and the stumbling blocks you encountered along the way.

NICOLE HAISLETT
Winner of three Olympic gold medals in swimming

The trait that I have seen over the years that I can pass on to the young kids is how to take a winning attitude and take it to the extreme of cockiness—not overboard—but right to the brink of cockiness so that you seem so confident about each other as a unit that it translates into wins.

————

MICHAEL JORDAN
Led the Chicago Bulls to six NBA championships

It does not really matter who I play, because all I can do is play the best I can. I focus on my own game.

ANNIKA SORENSTAM

*LPGA Player of the Year and first woman to break 60
in an LPGA tournament*

If you leave
yourself an out,
you're setting yourself up
for failure.

MICHAEL WEISS

Two-time U.S. figure skating champion

Y ou've got to be ready to play hockey every night. When things go bad, they go bad. Soon as the game's over, you have got to forget about it. Learn from your mistakes and move on.

MATHIEU SCHNEIDER
Los Angeles Kings defenseman

I think winning is a learned behavior. I put a lot of weight behind the fact you have experience, because I really think it eliminates the unknown. You know what it's like.

JOE TORRE
Manager of the New York Yankees

The rules of cycling also apply to life. Take care of yourself. Set goals. Learn from the experts. Share your wisdom. Be prepared.

KAREN BLISS LIVINGSTON

Top cyclist

You've got to have patience and take what's given you. At the same time, you can't be afraid to pull the trigger.

———

JERRY BAILEY

Hall of Fame jockey and four-time winner of the Eclipse Award as nation's most outstanding jockey

It's real easy to gain a focus and concentration when you feel like you're in a must-win game.

SCOTT BROSIUS

New York Yankee third baseman

I know I give up some things by not wrestling with women, but I'm getting amazing mental toughness getting my butt kicked every day.

PATRICIA MIRANDA
Lone female on Stanford University's men's wrestling team

When you use the words "mystique" and "aura," those are dancers in a nightclub, not something we concern ourselves with on the field. It comes down to nine on nine for nine innings. Whoever plays mistake-free baseball is going to win.

CURT SCHILLING

Arizona Diamondbacks pitcher talking about playing against the Yankees in the World Series

I can't say I always expected I was going to win, but I felt I had the power to win. I was definitely born with the ability to go out and concentrate and focus on what I was doing. Nothing could change it because my mind was set on what I was going to do.

NANCY LOPEZ
Member of the LPGA Hall of Fame

I live on trust.
I live on a handshake.
I don't believe in paper.
I believe in people.

ABE POLLIN
Owner of the Washington Wizards NBA team

I really have the
amateur spirit.
Above all, it's the
quest for performance;
to achieve goals.

JEANNIE LONGO-CIPRELLI
Winner of thirty Olympic and World Championship
medals in cycling

Regardless of how confident and poised you are, there's something to having been there before.

BRIAN BILLICK

Head coach of the NFL Baltimore Ravens

S ometimes you win, sometimes you don't. It's a subjective sport. Inside, all that matters is if you felt you skated the best you could.

SARAH HUGHES

2002 Olympic gold medalist in figure skating

Sometimes you have to win ugly.

VINNIE TESTEVERDE
New York Jets quarterback

This award means more than anything I have ever received or ever will receive as a baseball player. Because to win this award, it will not matter how many wins or strikeouts I have. I will have made a difference in people's lives.

CURT SCHILLING

Arizona Diamondbacks pitcher who won the 2001 Roberto Clemente Award for community service

My parents never told me, "You can't do that." They always said, "Go for it."

LORI KANE

LPGA champion from Canada

There's a certain feeling that prevails, that come hell or high water we know how to rally our collective energies together to play, and to defend this championship. There's a subtle thing, and it's not overconfidence. It's more an abiding reliance on each other and the team, that's playing together and playing to the best of our abilities.

PHIL JACKSON
Head coach of the Los Angeles Lakers

I believe people run marathons every day of their lives in one way or another, and we need to remember to give ourselves the finishers' medals we deserve.

ZOE KOPLOWITZ

Finished twelve New York City Marathons, always taking more than twenty-four hours because she suffers from multiple sclerosis and walks the course with the help of two special canes

We're all masters of adaptation. Distractions bother you, but you still have to go to work. You adapt and move on.

LINDY INFANTE

Former head coach of the NFL Indianapolis Colts

I do a lot of mental preparation, lots of visualization. I always take a nap before a game, that's when I visualize my shots, my free throws. That gets me ready. I see the shots I'm going to make and I see them going in.

NATALIE WILLIAMS
WNBA and U.S. national team forward

If you don't have
butterflies, it's because
you know you have
no chance.

PAUL AZINGER

Member of the 2001 Ryder Cup team

Some people think failure is the end of the world. Failure should be a challenge. If you don't get knocked on your ass ten or fifteen times in your life, you'll never reach your level of excellence.

NICK BOLLETTIERI
Renowned tennis coach

It's time now that we act like we know how to win, and that it's not a surprise, and that we handle it with dignity.

RALPH FRIEDGEN

Head football coach of University of Maryland

I close my eyes and see the shot. I look at the ball and see the type of shot I have in my mind. I see it fly and I see it land. It's a way of seeing the result before you do it. I visualize the end result.

ANNIKA SORENSTAM
Three-time women's U.S. Open golf champion

I believe in the philosophy of staying hungry. If you have a dream and it becomes a reality, don't stay satisfied too long. Make up a new dream and hunt after that one and turn it into a reality.

ARNOLD SCHWARZENEGGER
Winner of 13 world bodybuilding titles and former chairman of the President's Council on Physical Fitness

It appears that whenever you're in a ball game, that game, at that moment, is as big as it gets. However, no one game defines what kind of coach, or team, or program you are.

FRANK SOLICH
Head football coach of the University of Nebraska

The mark of a good team
is how it reacts when
things aren't going
in its favor.

CHRIS OSGOOD
Goalie for the NHL New York Islanders

I don't believe in luck. It seems like the good teams, the teams that are dynasties, have that certain edge, and the balls fall their way.

THOMAS RONGEN

Head coach of D.C. United soccer team

I've always embraced the positiveness of training with the right people and being with the right coach.

DEENA DROSSIN

Four-time U.S. cross-country champion and 2000 Olympian

I've learned if you have the chance, you'd better take it. Life's too precious. I always tell my players, "Enjoy the now."

GARY WILLIAMS

Head basketball coach of the University of Maryland, 2002 NCAA champions

I've always been told, "You're too nice. You can't win." But I've never believed that you had to be nasty to be a winner. I am not concerned with beating other people. I've discovered that the battle is with yourself.

CHIP BECK
PGA golfer

Every sport is about the fighting spirit, about winning as much as possible. You have to learn how to win and how to lose. Yes, you even have to learn how to win, how not to become arrogant, because concealed within each victory is the seed for the next defeat if you make a mistake.

HEINRICH VON PIERER
CEO of Siemens AG and avid tennis player

My motivation is trying to prove everyone wrong who said I couldn't do it. I've been that way my whole life, but failure's my biggest fear.

ZACH THOMAS
Pro Bowl linebacker for the Miami Dolphins

It's great to show people that you don't have to put an age limit on your dreams, and you don't have to be a teenager to win a gold medal

----

DARA TORRES
At thirty-three, became the oldest U.S. swimmer to win an
Olympic gold medal at the 2000 Sydney Games

I fight every day.
But who said a fight has
to be tongue and feet?
You fight by showing
you can overcome.

MOOKIE WILSON
New York Mets coach

Failure is only permanent if you allow it to be. Your future is not measured by your past. Keep hoping. Keep believing.

TRACEY STEWART

Wife of PGA golfer Payne Stewart, who died in a plane crash

You have to have the mentality of executing your game when you don't feel like there's a lot of hope. I think the best feeling is when somebody pushes you to the limit and you dig down a little bit extra. By the same token, you also need a little luck. Sometimes they come together.

ANDRE AGASSI ·
Winner of all four tennis Grand Slams

You have to believe you're great. You have to have an air about you. My success wasn't because I was a great talent, but because I wanted it more than anybody. Every time I step on that field, I want to prove I'm the best player in the league.

BRETT FAVRE
*Quarterback for the Green Bay Packers
and three-time MVP*

We play because we love the game, we love each other, and we love to win.

MIA HAMM

Star of the U.S. women's national soccer team and the WUSA Freedom

You never want to lose the respect of the guys you play with, because that's everything.

———

TOM BRADY

Quarterback for the 2002 Super Bowl–winning
New England Patriots

So many people get their identity through sports, and we have to remember that's what they do and not who they are.

PAT SUMMITT

Renowned Tennessee women's basketball coach

It was all or nothing.
I was so close to losing
I figured I had
nothing more to lose.

JENNIFER CAPRIATI

2001 Australian Open champion describing her reaction to being down match point four times in the second set

You may not
win them over
but if you hang around
long enough
you'll wear them out.

PHIL SIMMS

*Former quarterback of the New York Giants
and TV analyst*

The little things add up. All the nitpicky things that most teams let go in the end can make a difference in a tight game. Not being late for the bus, making sure your shirt is tucked in—stupid things that don't matter at all add up to make a professional environment. When push comes to shove, it's the little things that make a difference.

―――――――――

ANN COOK
WUSA player

When you're on top of your game, you don't take anything for granted. Every at-bat for me is important. I don't want to leave anything at the plate when I walk away.

SAMMY SOSA

Star slugger for the Chicago Cubs

There's no substitute for hard work. If you work hard and you prepare yourself as an athlete and you're in great shape, you might get beat, but you'll never lose. Losing is when you're not prepared. On any given day you'll get beat, because that's just sports.

NANCY LIEBERMAN-CLINE
Basketball legend and television commentator

In football,
as in business and life,
it's not over until
you say it's over.
You always have a
chance to win.

ALEX SPANOS
Owner of the San Diego Chargers